Th
Happy
to Stay
Happy

**THE AWESOME POWER
OF LEARNED OPTIMISM**

Becca Anderson

mango

Published by Mango Publishing Group, a division of Mango
Media Inc.

Cover Design: Roberto Nuñez
Layout & Design: Morgane Leoni

For permission requests, please contact the publisher at:
Mango Publishing Group
2850 Douglas Road, 3rd Floor
Coral Gables, FL 33134 U.S.A.
info@mango.bz

For special orders, quantity sales, course adoptions and corporate sales,
please email the publisher at sales@mango.bz. For trade and wholesale
sales, please contact Ingram Publisher Services at:
customer.service@ingramcontent.com or +1.800.509.4887.

Think Happy to Stay Happy: The Awesome Power of Learned Optimism

Library of Congress Cataloging
ISBN: (p) 978-1-63353-731-6, (e) 978-1-63353-730-9
Library of Congress Control Number: 2017962616
BISAC - OCC010000 BODY, MIND & SPIRIT / Mindfulness & Meditation
    - SEL016000 SELF-HELP / Personal Growth / Happiness

Printed in the United States of America

Contents

Foreword

Choose happiness. This is *your* life: only you can truly control your choices, and choosing happiness is the best way to achieve being the best *you* that you can be. Here are some suggestions for how you can ensure happiness in your life:

- Be the best you can be by your own standards.

- Surround yourself with people who inspire you and make you feel good.

- Focus on what you have, not on what you lack.

- Remember: optimism trumps pessimism.

- Smile often and genuinely.

- Be honest...to yourself and to others.

- Help others.

- Embrace your past, live in the present, and look forward to what is yet to come.

INTRODUCTION: CHANGE YOUR THINKING TO CHANGE YOUR LIFE

We all need reminders now and then. You don't leap out of bed every day, knowing you are amazing and about to have an incredible day. All of us have a lot of demands, pressures, to-do lists, and responsibilities, so we find ourselves rushing around and working hard to please others. Most of the time, you find yourself at the back of your own bus, having made everyone else happy but your own darn self. Then you go and beat yourself up about it.

Let's stop that, shall we?

I'm here to remind you that you are pretty darn great. I had to learn to remind myself of that, but you know what? It feels pretty darn good. It is even kind of addictive, in the best possible way. While this might seem like a fluffy little exercise, it actually runs quite deep and will serve you the rest of your life. There are reasons we need esteem boosters here and there: we pick up scars along the way and get bumps and bruises in the wake of daily life. If you had a bad childhood, you have these old "tapes" from poor parenting that loop around in your brain on an unconscious level, saying: "You'll never amount to anything. You're not good at sports. Your sister has a much better singing voice than you, so we're sending her to music camp and you can stay behind and babysit." Even really nice moms and dads perpetrate parenting errors that leave marks on the souls of their children.

If you find yourself feeling overwhelmed and drained by the busyness of life and its oh-so-many demands, you need to stop in your tracks and do an attitude adjustment—or more specifically, a "gratitude adjustment." Whenever you have gotten to this point, you need some "me-TLC" and a dose of radical self-care. Chances are, your very wonderfulness might have led you to give and give and give some more. Now, you need to give and give and *give to yourself.* You need to soak up the glory of your very being and remember that you are an amazing, awesome person, someone who deserves all the good things our world has to offer!

The world is changing all around us with ever-increasing speed, making most of us feel like we have no control. We are so busy doing and being productive and bullet-journaling our way through life that it seems like we might be riding on the back of our own bus. I consider myself a Positive Living and Affirmation Queen, despite having been to the edge of overwhelm and back again! While on my journey, I have gathered a lot of wisdom and my big takeaway is this:

If you affirm yourself every day, you can rule the world. More importantly, you can live a life filled with love, joy, fulfillment, and satisfaction, thanks to your own positive self-regard.

Through the art of daily self-affirmation, you can take control of your own destiny and create your ideal life. If that sounds easy, it can be—but you need the discipline to reflect upon a positive affirmation each day. These affirmations are a mindfulness practice that will strengthen your self-esteem. It's like a muscle: the more you practice self-affirmation, the stronger your confidence and sense of self will be. *Think Happy to Stay Happy* is the ultimate motivating, encouraging, and uplifting book to enjoy and share. These wise words and affirmative sayings have the power to touch our hearts, make us laugh, and alleviate our stress, while realizing the vast potential life has to offer. Grouped together, these quips, quotes, and "power thoughts" can help you deal with everything life throws at you, with élan and a spring in your step. Simply put, you'll be too blessed to be stressed!

Author Note:
The Art of Self-Affirmation:
How to Use This Book

Pick up the book, randomly open to a quote and let those words be your guiding thought for the day. If you are *really* resonating to this power thought, keep using it every day and let it become your mantra.

Use these inspired ideas in speeches, pin them on your bulletin board, put them in your email signature, make them your Twitter handle, or post them on your social media. Hey, if it is your favorite ever Big Thought, get a tattoo on your inner wrist where you see it all the time and are reminded of your personal worth and of the great big, beautiful world we all live in.

Read a few and really "power up" for your day; sort of like a booster shot in word form. If you are getting ready to do a presentation, a sales pitch, an interview for your dream job, your next YouTube taping, or any very important date, this affirmation can be the wind in your sails.

Always remember this: *you have to think happy to stay happy!*

big hugs
—Becca Anderson

BE A "DAY LIFTER!"

Think about the things that motivate and inspire you and how you can inspire others. What lifts you up? Who fills you with hope and happiness? Cultivate these qualities in yourself and pay attention to who are your "day-lifters." You may be surprised!

"BE SOMEBODY WHO MAKES
EVERYBODY FEEL LIKE
A SOMEBODY."

—BRAD MONTAGUE

Random Acts of Love

Think about how you can create little moments of happiness for others: helping a friend plant her garden, buying an extra coffee for your coworker, paying the toll for the car behind you on the bridge, even taking your kids to a movie. All those little things can add up to *big* joy.

LIVE GENTLY WITH YOURSELF AND OTHERS.

BE A GOOD IN THE WORLD

Take stock of your day-to-day life. Are you giving to others, or are you a little out of balance, where your work and your immediate family get 99 percent of what you offer the world? You can change that in one day. Donate more of your time or money to a charity. Supporting a cause will help keep you informed about social issues and can strengthen your sense of well-being while benefitting others in the process.

WHAT DID YOU DO TO SAVE THE WORLD TODAY?

MAKE CONTACT

Put down your smartphone and make eye contact.
Person-to-person. Nowadays, I consider that a major
acts of kindness and courtesy.

BELIEVE IN YOURSELF AND
YOU WILL BE UNSTOPPABLE.

In Your Own Backyard

Make a list of small things you can do around your house, neighborhood, and place of work to conserve energy and water, stop waste, and up the recycling.

Then start doing them.

BEGIN ANYWHERE.

Spread Joy at the Office

Make a point of smiling at everyone you encounter and cross paths with today. Such a simple thing can mean an awful lot.

WORK LIKE A BOSS.

Scatter Happiness All Around

Being a source of happiness in another person's day can be extremely rewarding. To put this into practice, try thinking of how someone has turned a bad day of yours into a joyful one. Maybe a friend called just to check in on you, a family member gave you encouraging advice, or a stranger was courteous and friendly. There are many way you can plant the seed of happiness today—whether it be wishing someone a great day, complimenting someones talents, or helping someone without being asked. You never know how much another person may need it. Scatter the seed of happiness wherever you go and watch it grow!

THE BEST PART ABOUT LIFE?
EVERY MORNING YOU HAVE
A NEW OPPORTUNITY TO
BECOME A HAPPIER VERSION
OF YOURSELF.

GIVE GLADNESS TO OTHERS

When you talk to someone, show them how *glad* you are to see them. Say it with words, say it with a smile, say it with a hug (or a warm handshake). Even if you're feeling glum yourself, you can still be a beacon of gladness for someone else. And studies have shown that smiling makes you happier!

"In normal life we
hardly realize how
much more we receive
than we give, and life
cannot be rich without
such gratitude."

—Dietrich Bonhoeffer

WHAT THE WORLD NEEDS NOW

There's no moment like the present. Don't wait to do something you know in your heart is right. Take a risk, big or small. Strike up a conversation with someone at the bus stop, ask a friend or coworker how they're doing, show someone you care. Or maybe you want to start something bigger, locally or globally. Organize a block party or neighborhood barbeque, start a Facebook or MeetUp group around a shared interest, sign up to volunteer for a charity or cause you believe in. There's no day like today!

"NEVER ALLOW WAITING TO
BECOME A HABIT. LIVE YOUR
DREAMS AND TAKE RISKS.
LIFE IS HAPPENING NOW."

—PAULO COELHO

Learn the Language of Kindness

Learn a new language. Or become more fluent in your less-dominant language if you are already bilingual. The more people you can communicate with, the more valuable you are to working opportunities as well as opening yourself up to new people and cultures. A friend of mine recently took a volunteer vacation where he taught English to orphans and abandoned children in Liberia. He said he enjoyed every minute and wants to do this every year, as he loved working with the kids. As he told me this story, his smile was at least a mile wide!

Beautiful minds
inspire others.

The Little Things Count

Do little things for others: hold a door open and let someone go before you; invite the person with only one item to check out ahead of you at the grocery store. So many people rush through life and don't consider the feelings of others; I think this is due to our over-busyness. Nowadays, a simple gesture can be a good reminder for us all, myself included. Take your time, look around you, and ask, "How can I help someone today?" In the end, you are also helping yourself just as much.

YOUR GREATNESS IS NOT WHAT YOU HAVE, IT'S WHAT YOU GIVE.

Free Hugs for All!

Be an indiscriminate hugger. When I first moved to California, I was a bit taken aback by all the hugging. Now, I love it. Be a hugger. A hug is a mutual act of love and affection that induces feelings of comfort, contentment, and security. Hugs are one of the most beautifully human things we can do.

I REALIZED THERE IS
NO SHAME IN BEING
HONEST. THERE IS
NO SHAME IN BEING
VULNERABLE. IT'S THE
BEAUTY OF BEING HUMAN.

DON'T FORGET THE SENSELESS ACTS OF BEAUTY!

Anne Herbert, the poet-artist who coined the term "Random Acts of Kindness," also implored us to add prettiness to the world. There are so many ways to do this: plant flowers, pick up trash, or paint a lovely mural for the entire neighborhood's pleasure.

WHAT BEAUTY CAN YOU
BRING TO THE WORLD?

No Strings Attached

Write down the things that someone has given you, no strings attached, for which you are grateful. It can be an old sofa, some sound advice, or a lift to the airport. Now list ten things that you would like to give someone yourself, and see how many of those things you can cross off in a week.

Examples:

- Drive a friend to the airport

- Carry groceries for an elder to their car

- Babysit for a relative

- Buy a friend a cup of coffee

- Volunteer at a soup kitchen

No one is you and that
is your power. We rise by
lifting others.

MAKE AMENDS

It's never too late to say you're sorry. Apologize to someone you wronged in the past, especially if you stopped communicating because of the issue. By admitting fault and letting them know how sorry you are to have hurt them, you are taking responsibility for your actions and proving that you care enough for them to make things right. However bad you felt over the problem, you will feel five times better after making peace.

BETTER AN "OOPS!" THAN A "WHAT IF?"

SHARE THE LOVE!

Tell someone close to you how much you love them, even if you're sure they already know. You can be general, or specific. Is there some quirk about your loved one that makes you smile, that little something they might not realize you love about them?

"I AM NOT WEIRD,
I AM LIMITED EDITION."

—J. T. GEISSINGER, WICKED SEXY

ALWAYS REMEMBER, IT'S NOT ALL ABOUT YOU

We don't always have to donate time and energy to other parts of the world. Sometimes help is needed much closer to home. Is a parent, sibling, spouse, or friend having a difficult time? Let them experience that loving feeling and help lift their spirits. Invite them to coffee or to dinner, surprise them with a simple gift, and take them somewhere they like. Lean forward and listen closely. As the StoryCorps oral history project tagline says, "Listening is an Act of Love."

"You're always one
decision away from a
totally different life."
—Mark Batterson

LIVE WITH PURPOSE AND MEANING

When we live from our values, we feel happier. This isn't flash happiness; it isn't the kind that lasts for a few minutes when we get a new toy or enjoy a concert. This is the kind of happiness that lingers in the background of our lives and keeps you sleeping well at night.

Only when you learn to truly love yourself can you give your heart to another.

LOVE YOURSELF FIRST,
BECAUSE THAT'S WHO YOU'LL
BE SPENDING THE REST OF
YOUR LIFE WITH.

THE ART OF MAKING A LIFE

Set some goals. Stay quiet about them. Celebrate
your accomplishments: "You did good!"

"WE MAKE A LIVING BY
WHAT WE GET, BUT WE MAKE
A LIFE BY WHAT WE GIVE."

—WINSTON CHURCHILL

WHAT IS YOUR PERSONAL MISSION?

Challenge yourself. Life is a process, and during that process you should get to know yourself better, surprise yourself, challenge yourself. If you go through life without trying something new, you are not doing yourself justice. Discover your true potential and maybe more than just your life will benefit.

SELF-CONFIDENCE IS
A SUPER POWER. ONCE
YOU START TO BELIEVE IN
YOURSELF, MAGIC
STARTS HAPPENING!

THINK "BEST-CASE SCENARIO" ALL THE TIME

Many people overanalyze situations, psych themselves out, and only consider the worst-case scenarios. I, for one, am guilty as charged. Let's start each day on a positive footing and make a list of your "best-case scenarios." What are the best things that could possibly happen to you? To your family? To the world? Have fun with this and think big!

"You gain strength, courage, and confidence by every experience in which you stop to look fear in the face."

—Eleanor Roosevelt

Do You Know How Great You Are?

Compliment someone today, and mean it. A genuine compliment can boost someone's confidence, and that is a great feeling. If you like your coworker's blouse or new haircut (or both!), tell her. Open and honest communication works wonders for developing relationships and makes everybody's day a little bit nicer.

A BAD ATTITUDE CAN
LITERALLY BLOCK LOVE,
BLESSINGS, AND DESTINY
FROM FINDING YOU.
DON'T BE THE REASON YOU
DON'T SUCCEED.

YOUR GOALS WILL GROW YOU

Make a list of short-term goals you would like to achieve by the end of the year, month, or even week. As you accomplish your goals, give gratitude for the effort, inspiration, people, and other factors that helped you along the way. My goal is to see how I can give more to those around me, near and far. I know you have your own aspirations!

BE THE HERO
OF YOUR OWN STORY.

Yes, You Can

Remove the word "can't" from your vocabulary and think about what is actually holding you back—fear, reluctance, pride? Once you stop talking yourself out of taking a risk or making a difficult decision, life will open up for you and so will your mind.

THE ONLY PERSON WHO
IS GOING TO GIVE YOU
SECURITY AND THE LIFE YOU
WANT IS YOU.

LIST YOUR LIFE

Instead of writing up and crossing things off of a "bucket list," create a "life list." Let your hopes, dreams, fears, and thoughts spill out of you and into this list. Next to each entry, write down how that emotion or fear makes you feel—does it hold you back or empower you? This task will put you on the road to self-discovery. Knowing who you are is important in order to have relationships with others. The ancient Greeks had it right when they said: "Know thyself."

YOUR ATTITUDE DETERMINES YOUR DIRECTION.

ASK "HOW ARE YOU?" AND MEAN IT!

Ask someone how their day is going and make their reply into a conversation. Sometimes people want to talk more than they let on, and your interest will show them you care. One day, you'll get the chance to tell some kind-hearted person exactly how *you* are. Your answer to that question might not always be pretty but it will feel wonderful to be heard.

OLD WAYS WON'T OPEN
NEW DOORS.

Today Is a Great Day: Let Yourself Enjoy It

As the wise sage Charlie Chaplin said, "A day without laughter is a day wasted." Laughter and good humor are infectious. Sharing a funny story or memory with others helps to bind people together, increasing happiness and intimacy between friends, acquaintances, and loved ones. According to helpguide.org, laughter triggers happiness and can strengthen the immune system, boost energy, relieve physical and emotional pain, and battle the effects of stress. Today is a great day, let yourself enjoy it.

Don't feel guilty
for doing what's best
for you.

ACCENTUATE THE POSITIVE

Finding positives and accentuating them is the easiest way to turn those proverbial frowns upside down and gray skies back to blue. Try catching someone doing something right for a change, not something wrong. Giving praise for a job well done lifts all parties involved and is the easiest way to say "thank you" and show you really mean it.

TRUST THE TIMING
OF YOUR LIFE.

Be the Light on Dark Days

Sometimes we all feel deflated or overwhelmed, someone or something hurts us or disappoints us, or we hear bad news about a loved one's medical condition. On those days, when you feel your light has gone out, remember there is always a glimmer of hope and something to be thankful for. Albert Schweitzer said it well: "Sometimes our light goes out, but is blown again into instant flame by an encounter with another human being. Each of us owes the deepest thanks to those who have rekindled this inner light."

A GRATEFUL HEART IS A MAGNET FOR MIRACLES.

MAKE TIME FOR GRATITUDE EVERY DAY

When we begin a daily practice of recognizing the positive events that occur and the pleasant encounters we have with others, we start noticing more things to be thankful for as the days pass. Perhaps it's someone who holds the door for you at the supermarket, the nice conversation you have with a stranger while at the coffee shop, or a hug with someone you love. These are the small moments, and often the ones we forget. Savor their beauty and what they tell you about humankind—that we do live amongst many good people.

ANGER?
GRUDGES?
LET GO AND MOVE ON.

Look at Everything in a New Way

Simply reframe your perception: each of us has dreams that for one reason or another we do not achieve. And we all make choices that perhaps were not the best we could have made. Yet, rather than allowing regret to overtake us, we must see and celebrate all the other goals we've accomplished and positive choices we've made.

Human nature so often leads us to perceive the one negative in a sea of positives. But, we can retrain ourselves to acknowledge both, learn the lessons embedded in our mistakes, and allow ourselves to see and feel pride in the beauty we are capable of. All it takes is a little shift. You'll see!

WHEN LIFE PUTS YOU
IN TOUGH SITUATIONS,
DON'T SAY "WHY ME?"
SAY "TRY ME."

GOSSIP MAKES US ALL UNHAPPY

Avoid listening to or spreading gossip. This is a really hard one in our tabloid society, but it is something really to be avoided. For one thing, it spreads negative energy all around. Say something nice instead. And mean it!

THE WORLD IS GONNA
JUDGE YOU NO MATTER
WHAT YOU DO, SO LIVE YOUR
LIFE THE WAY YOU REALLY
WANT TO.

Do What You Say You're Gonna Do

Make this the guiding principle of your life. Really commit. Saying you'll do something and actually doing it are two very different things. Commit to something you've been meaning to do and take the first step today.

It's on.
Time to make
the magic happen.

OFFER UNCONDITIONAL POSITIVE REGARD

Be accepting. No matter a person's race, age, culture, or sexual orientation, accept everyone for who they are. Embrace the beauty of humanity and how different everyone is. By opening your eyes and mind to the possibility of love and friendship, new people will flow into your life and change your perspective in miraculous ways.

TREAT PEOPLE WELL.
AND YOU WILL BE
TREATED WELL.

PRACTICE SIMPLE ACTS OF GOODNESS

Get acquainted with the power of simple human kindness—simple acts of goodness every day. When at the grocery store, return the cart, help the elderly man struggling with his bags. Open doors for people; say "Hello!" with a smile. Every day and in every way choose to take the high road in your travels. The view is much more beautiful from up top!

Sometimes the smallest
step in the right
direction ends up being
the biggest step
of your life.

LIFE IS TOO SHORT TO NOT HAVE GOOD COFFEE

Get your cup of Joe and help orphans in Kamba, Kenya, with World Vision's twelve-ounce whole-bean coffee set, complete with a hand-carved olivewood scoop. Check out their website; worldvision.org.

GET UP.
GET COFFEE.
GET ON WITH IT.

WHAT ARE YOU HERE TO DO IN THIS LIFE?

"To Be of Use," Marge Piercy's marvelous poem, suggests something about the human condition—that we all long to be useful, to help, to work together towards a common goal. This is surely the best part of the human spirit. Meditate upon this:

What is my true purpose? What am I here to do in this life?

I recommend that you contemplate this question deeply and for a very long time—days, weeks, months, and years even. Let the answer speak through your service to others.

You are allowed to be
both a masterpiece and
a work in progress
simultaneously.

THE VIRTUES OF KINDNESS, GENEROSITY, PATIENCE, AND HOPE

I love the old-fashioned ideas of virtues such as kindness and generosity a *lot*. I am determined to develop my patience muscle so it gets stronger all the time. Here is a big one for me; to learn to have patience with difficult people. (And realize I may be one myself and not know it!) This is not only a good deed for the person you are exhibiting patience towards, but it is also a good deed for yourself! Imagine that, a good deed for yourself! For example, when someone is purposely trying to push your buttons by doing something or saying something rude, you can choose to act with patience and understanding instead of anger. This will benefit you by keeping your blood pressure low and your stress levels low as well—which we know are two health issues that many people are suffering from today. My wise woman friend B. J. Gallagher says, "Difficult people are the ones we learn the most from."

Be kind.
Even on your bad days.

Just Say Yes

I (re)learned this truly vital lesson from *Imperfect Spirituality* blogger and author Polly Campbell: Once today say "yes" to something unexpected that comes into your life.

Know that you are enough to handle whatever emerges from the "yes." Know that you have the whole Universe supporting you. Believe that you will have a good time and learn something that you need to know. Exercise your faith by taking the Universe up on the good things that come your way and practice your optimism by believing that there is more to come. Just. Say. Yes.

EVERY DAY IS A CHANCE
TO CHANGE YOUR LIFE.

Don't Just Go Through It, Grow Through It

An attitude of gratitude can make a profound difference in our day-to-day lives, yet, as we all come to know, not every day is filled with all good things. We each endure difficult passages: illnesses, money trouble, work woes, relationship issues, the loss of a loved one, and countless others. These are the vicissitudes of life. However, it is the attitude you bring to each situation that makes all the difference. Share what you learned from others from your life lessons and offer it if you think it can be of help to a fellow traveler who is walking a hard path.

LIFE IS TOUGH,
MY DARLING,
BUT SO ARE YOU.

REWIRE YOUR BRAIN TO BE MORE POSITIVE

Neuropsychiatrist David Amen, MD, posits that thoughts carry physical properties and that the properties of negative thoughts can be detrimental to your leading a healthy, happy life. To overturn these negative effects, he prescribes thinking more positively, maintaining that by doing so, you can change the way your brain works and in turn change your life for the better.

There's a million fish in the sea, but I'm a mermaid.

REMEMBER TO BE KIND TO YOURSELF, TOO

Make a commitment to yourself to refrain from negative self-talk. Be kind to yourself and focus on the traits you like rather than the ones you don't. The extremely wise Dawna Markova, the author of some of my favorite books, including *I Will Not Die an Unlived Life*, says, "Your soul remembers when you put yourself down; it imprints upon you. Never do this. Self-compassion is key to a life well-lived."

HEY, LITTLE FIGHTER, SOON
THINGS WILL BE BRIGHTER.

Be of Good Cheer

Open the doors for everyone: young, old, everyone in between. Simply because it is a very, very, very nice thing to do!

If I ever let my head
down it will just be to
admire my shoes.

Be Happy For Others (and Let Them Know It!)

When someone tells you their good news, be excited for them and show your enthusiasm. Sometimes we envy the good things that happen to others, but it is better to focus on how happy this person is and allow their joy to become yours as well. In fact, I think it is okay to gush!

REGARDLESS OF HOW
ANYONE ELSE FEELS ABOUT
ME, I AM GOING TO
CHOOSE TO BE HAPPY
AND TO COMPLETELY LOVE
MYSELF TODAY.

Simply Reframe Your Perceptions

At some point in our lives, unfortunately, we will face setbacks or failure. Think of these experiences, however, as opportunities for growth and learning. If we never faced challenges, we would not grow stronger or gain wisdom through the conflict. Further, if everything was easy, the important things would not hold so much meaning to us. Learn to embrace these learning experiences and to deeply cherish what is important. Remember, life is not happening to you, it is happening for you.

You are magic. Don't
ever apologize for the
fire in you.

Find Joy in Gratitude

The easiest way to turn your state of mind upwards is, simply, to give thanks. Expressing gratitude for your blessings will not only cause your mind to feel joy, but will spread it out into the world. Reminding yourself of all you have, instead of reflecting on what you don't, will shift your perspective in the most positive of ways. The writer and activist Alice Walker once said, "'Thank you' is the best prayer anyone can say." It is truly the simplest way to "express extreme gratitude, humility, [and] understanding." Each day, think of at least five things you are grateful for, and share this gratitude and joy with your loved ones.

"The miracle of
gratitude is that it shifts
your perception to such
an extent that it changes
the world you see."

—Dr. Robert Holden

ACTIONS REALLY ARE LOUDER THAN WORDS

Pay attention to the body language of others around you and offer assistance if they need it. Someone could be having a bad day, and one person noticing and helping him or her could make a big difference. Be that person.

You can make
a big difference in
somebody's life.

WEED NEGATIVITY OUT OF YOUR MIND (AND OUT OF YOUR LIFE)

Take control. You are the ringleader of the circus that is your life. Take control of your choices, be dominant rather than submissive, and allow happiness into your life while banning anything negative from your mind. Put yourself at the top of your to-do list every single day, and the rest will fall into place. Overcome obstacles. Life throws many unexpected things are way. View these things as challenges that will make you stronger rather than weaker. Focus on the positives in each situation; don't let yourself give up.

KNOW YOUR WORTH.

Love Notes

Leave encouraging, inspiring, or funny notes/quotes in a library book or other random places (without littering or defiling public property!). A simple note pinned to a bulletin board, taped to a column, or written in chalk on the sidewalk may influence in wonderful ways—plus, you'll be like a secret agent, bringing happiness to others. The Art of Getting Started is a website with fun examples that might give you an idea; artofgettingstarted.com.

Try to love yourself
as much as you want
someone else to.

Make New Happy Memories

Learn to be alone and to like it. There is nothing more freeing and empowering than learning to enjoy your own company.

Go on vacation by yourself. Pick a town, state, or country that you have always wanted to go to and go there, alone! Think about it: you can make your own schedule, wake up when you want, stay out, stay in, and eat what you feel like…. This is your chance at making a memory that will last you a lifetime and add to the story of your life.

SHE NEEDED A HERO, SO THAT'S WHAT SHE BECAME.

REACH OUT

Make plans to go to a local nursing home and visit an elderly resident who isn't talking with or sitting next to anyone. Receiving extra one-on-one attention can be very rewarding for the resident, and you'll be surprised how interesting their life has been once you start talking with them. Especially when holidays are coming, think of those who might not have family nearby and who would love good company this time of year. Nine times out of ten, you will end up receiving much more than you gave to these elders who have so much to offer: wisdom, stories, advice, and love.

"One looks back with appreciation to the brilliant teachers, but with gratitude to those who touched our human feelings."

—Carl Jung

The Happiness Plan

People seem to think embracing life means to jump off cliffs and kiss strangers. Maybe it's just slowly learning to love yourself.

Overcome obstacles. Life throws many unexpected things are way. View these things as challenges that will make you stronger rather than weaker. Focus on the positives in each situation: don't let yourself give up.

Wayne Dyer said: "Give yourself a gift of five minutes of contemplation in awe of everything you see around you. Go outside and turn your attention to the many miracles around you. This five-minute-a-day regimen of appreciation and gratitude will help you to focus on your life in awe."

Don't call it a dream.
Call it a plan.

When Was the Last Time You Were a Good Samaritan?

I have no doubt you can immediately be helpful to someone, somewhere. Doing a favor for someone without expecting something in return is the epitome of kindness and will earn you some karma points down the line (though don't expect any!). Sometimes helping others is the best way to help yourself, and anytime one of my friends is singing the blues, I will say, "Let's go serve some beans down at Glide Memorial Church! You still stop feeling sorry for yourself in the first sixty seconds."

"The best way to find
yourself is to lose
yourself in the service
of others."

—Mahatma Gandhi

MAKE A DIFFERENCE IN THE WORLD

Whether it be doing something for others or achieving a personal goal, taking the first step towards that is the best way to achieve it. If a friend is suffering, actively listening is the simplest way to show them that you are there for them, and that you care. If you wish to achieve a goal, think about the very first step you need to take to get there. Action is the best way to make a difference in the world and in your own life. Take the first step today!

"Life's most persistent
and urgent question
is 'What are you doing
for others?'"

—Martin Luther King, Jr.

SAY MY NAME

When meeting new people, make an effort to remember their name, so that when you address them, it's more personal, respectful, and will make a good impression on them. Everyone is important. When you see them the next time, greet them by name. So simple, so nice.

"Courtesies of a small and trivial character are the ones which strike deepest in the grateful and appreciating heart."

—Henry Clay

SELF-CARE IS A DIVINE RESPONSIBILITY

Take time out to take care of yourself. If you can't take a spa day, bake yourself a nice batch of cookies or enjoy a long bath. You deserve it! It's the intention that counts.

NOTHING IN NATURE
BLOOMS ALL YEAR; BE
PATIENT WITH YOURSELF.

Check In with Your Friends

Add a half hour to your day: get up a half hour earlier and use that time to reach out to people. This can be as easy as wishing a happy birthday to your Facebook contacts, making one meaningful phone call first thing in the morning, or writing a personal note to someone you have longed to be in contact with.

FRIENDS ARE SOME OF THE
GREAT LOVES OF OUR LIVES
AND A GREAT SOURCE
OF HAPPINESS.

SEEK OUT THE SHY

Rescue a wallflower. Most people know what it's like to go to a party and end up standing by yourself. If you see someone alone, mosey on over to them and strike up a conversation. Nine times out of ten, they will have the *most* interesting things to say out of anybody at the party or dance.

"The deepest craving of human nature is the need to be appreciated."

—William James

THINK GLOBALLY

Start a conversation with someone of a different culture, religion, or political views. Actively listen and respond. Becoming aware of someone else's points of view and personal journeys may enlighten how you think. Nowadays, people of different vantage points need to realize that we may worship or think differently, but we are people all the same. Be accepting and show it. For example, so many different cultures celebrate unique holidays. Why not find out more about these festivities and even attend some? It is a small world, after all. Learn more about it.

"The aim of life is
appreciation; there
is no sense in not
appreciating things;
and there is no sense
in having more of
them if you have less
appreciation of them."

—G.K. Chesterton

SHOWER THE PEOPLE YOU LOVE WITH LOVE

These days, so many of us don't spend enough time with our families. Instead of spending time sequestered in separate rooms watching television, playing video games, or browsing the Internet, call all family members into the same room and do something together.

You can also make a festive occasion into an opportunity to share the love! After a wedding or party, donate all of the flowers to a nursing home or hospital. If that's not an option, take those flowers to your place of work and fill the entire office with beauty and love.

LOVE MORE.

Naps Make Us Happy

Take a nap. Really. Naps aren't just for kids. With all the hustle and bustle that is life, it is easy to become rundown, overwhelmed, and exhausted. It's healthiest to nap for fifteen to thirty minutes in the late afternoon to early evening. Napping will help you feel more relaxed, reduce fatigue, increase alertness, and improve your mood, so give it a try!

BE YOURSELF TODAY, YOU
LOOK BEAUTIFUL LIKE THAT.

Share the Positive

When reading an online article that you find helpful, moving, or enlightening, take a moment to leave a positive comment on the bottom of the page—acknowledge the writer for their style or content, or even add some additional information that you have about the topic. The writer—and other readers—may appreciate what you have to say. If it inspires you, share it, too. I started subscribing to www.lifehacks.com, and every morning, I come in to read some truly excellent and uplifting ideas in my inbox. I share the very best ones, and I've have heard from Facebook friends and fellow Tweeps on Twitter that they love 'em. So, as the old saying goes, accentuate the positive!

LIVE LESS OUT OF HABIT AND
MORE OUT OF INTENT.

Teach What You Know

My family frequently wondered what I would ever do with an English degree, but one thing I *can* do is mentor a student in grammar and hopefully foster a love of reading, the benefits of which will last a lifetime. I suggest you check out the vast array of opportunities to each and to learn at Teach For America; teachforamerica.org.

"People become really quite remarkable when they start thinking that they can do things. When they believe in themselves, they have the first secret of success."

—Norman Vincent Peale

THE LITTLE THINGS IN LIFE

Bring homemade goodies to work. Many of us work five days a week with the same people, in the same office, for the same amount of hours. That's the routine. Shake things up, in a good way! What could be more uplifting than arriving at work to the sight and smell of baked goods or snacks? Make something that most people would enjoy, such as chocolate chip cookies or banana bread. The work environment will become more warm and inviting, and making others feel good is one of the true pleasures in life.

EVERY DAY YOU MAKE A
CHOICE. CHOOSE BADASS A
LITTLE MORE OFTEN.

Make Furry Friends

Studies show that pets provide both a psychological and physical boost to their owners, so donate to <u>petsfortheelderly.org</u> to help a senior get a dog or a cat. The unconditional love of a pet can make a life much sweeter.

BE THE ENERGY YOU WANT TO ATTRACT.

BE A KID FOR A DAY

Remember the good ol' days when you had more art projects than responsibilities? You can still embrace your inner child by spending the day with a young relative or your own child playing games, making crafts, and encouraging creativity. You may reawaken talents and interests you had long since repressed and may introduce your child to new interests along the way. Paint a picture together, read storybooks aloud, play dress up, and talk with them. This will create a strong bond between you two that will last a lifetime and make for great memories. Time is the most precious resource, and spending it with a young person is will have lasting, positive results on a young life.

"ALL HUMAN BEINGS
ARE ALSO DREAM BEINGS.
DREAMING TIES ALL
MANKIND TOGETHER."

—JACK KEROUAC

PASS ON THE PLEASURE OF READING

Drop off your old magazines at a retirement home, hospice, or other place where the residents or patients may enjoy them. At my place of work, we get large-print copies of our books sent in multiples so we keep one for our library, send one to the authors and share the others with our local retirement home. An elder Beat poet lives in my El Cerrito village for elders so I can drop off a collection of magazines and large-print books and sit down for tea and a nice chat. I leave having received much more than I brought to them.

A BOOK CAN CHANGE A LIFE.

Go Ahead and Make Someone's Day

Some shops (coffee, frozen yogurt, sandwich) have punch cards that offer a free product after a certain amount of purchases. When your punch card gets full, give it to someone in line behind you and surprise them with the free coffee, frozen yogurt, or sandwich!

"What sunshine is to flowers, smiles are to humanity. These are but trifles, to be sure; but, scattered along life's pathway, the good they do is inconceivable."

—Joseph Addison

OFFER UNCONDITIONAL POSITIVE REGARD

Be accepting. No matter a person's race, age, culture, or sexual orientation, accept everyone for who they are. Embrace the beauty of humanity and how different everyone is. By opening your eyes and mind to the possibility of love and friendship, new people will flow into your life and change your perspective in miraculous ways.

"APPRECIATION IS AN
ART AND A LIFESTYLE AND
A SOURCE OF HAPPINESS
AND FULFILLMENT."

—ROBERT LEFFLER

CONCLUSION:
YOUR GUIDE TO GLAD DAYS

The affirmations, quotes and ideas in this book are a set of tools for you to use in your self-development. They are for "inner work." And, you know what they say about happiness—that it's an "inside job," which is one hundred percent true. These suggestions vary widely from spiritual aspirations to very simple, straightforward, and practical ideas. Much has to do with adjusting your attitude. Depending on the day, it might be a slight adjustment or a major overhaul, but the more you practice daily affirmations, the fewer adjustments you'll need. One day, you will realize you have mastered the art of "thinking happy" and are looking at the bright side of life, every day. Incorporating this as a daily practice will build "mental muscle" and help you achieve the all-important optimistic way of thinking.

I very much like the idea of idea of undertaking the inner work of self-development and working your way to a better you. I am also a strong advocate for believing in yourself and loving yourself more each and every day. These are habits that can easily be reinforced by practices such as journaling, creating your own affirmations, and talking to yourself in the positive. I can see how some people might think I have gone through my life like a horse with blinders on, listening to the voices in my head: "You're doing great!" and "Today is going to be awesome!" Yes, I do affirm myself and ascribe to some woo-woo ideas about the life-changing power of positive thinking. But, here's my point—it works!

Like an engine driving you toward greater things, self belief brings you closers to your life's purpose, your personal mission, and will absolutely make you a happier camper. Daily affirmations help build the optimistic mindset. So, try it. Easy as pie and just as sweet.

DIY Affirmation Journaling Pages

DO YOU KNOW HOW GREAT YOU ARE?

....

....

....

....

....

....

....

....

....

....

....

LIST 5 GREAT THINGS ABOUT YOURSELF:

....

....

....

....

....

....

....

....

....

....

....

....

WRITE AN AFFIRMATION A DAY FOR THE NEXT WEEK:

....
....
....
....
....
....
....
....
....
....
....
....

WHAT IS YOUR PERSONAL MISSION STATEMENT FOR YOUR LIFE?

....

....

....

....

....

....

....

....

....

....

....

....

WHAT ARE YOUR BEST TRAITS?

....

....

....

....

....

....

....

....

....

....

....

....

List 5 things you are grateful for:

....

....

....

....

....

....

....

....

....

....

....

....

WRITE A LIST OF AFFIRMATIONS RELATED TO YOUR WORK:

....

....

....

....

....

....

....

....

....

....

....

....

WRITE A LIST OF AFFIRMATIONS RELATED TO YOUR RELATIONSHIPS:

....

....

....

....

....

....

....

....

....

....

....

....

We would love for you to share your affirmations with us, so feel free to contact author Becca Anderson at Info@Mango.bz. We wish you many blessings, much success, and all happiness!

ABOUT THE AUTHOR

Becca Anderson is a writer, gardener, and teacher living in the San Francisco Bay Area. Originally from Ohio, Becca's background in sustainability and landscaping inspired her to become a part of the seed-saving and seed-sharing community, with chapters across the U.S. and Canada. Becca Anderson credits her first-grade teacher as a great inspiration and runs several popular classes and workshops including "How to Put Your Passion on Paper." Anderson is currently at work on a book about the healing power of gardening.